Bowl Like a Pro:
The Secret Book of
the Masters

Table of Contents

How to Use This Book 3
Part 1: Introduction 5
   It Started One Fine Day... 5
   The Evolution of Bowling... 9
Part 2: Balls & Pins 11
   Selecting Your Bowling Balls 11
   Mastering Bowling Ball Cover Stocks 18
      Polyester Bowling Balls 18
      Urethane Bowling Balls 20
      Reactive Resin Bowling Balls 21
   Rack & Pins 22
   Bowling Shoes and Why They Count 26
   Maintenance Tips for Bowling Balls 29
Part 3: Play It Right 31
   Etiquette... Or How to Bowl Like a Sir/Madame 32
   The Scoring System in Bowling 38
   Gripping a Bowling Ball for the First Time 41
   Throwing Hooks 43
   Throwing Accurate Straight Shots 47
   Quick Points: The Essentials of Bowling 51
Part 4: Play It Smart 56
   Oil Patterns 56
   Mastering Spares 61
   Adjustment Guidelines 64
References 66

How to Use This Book

Bowl Like a Pro: The Secret Book of the Masters was written and designed for both beginners and intermediate players of the sport to aid them in improving their game through practical and down-to-earth instruction.

Part 1 deals with my personal history, and how I started in the sport. Also, it is in this part of the book I established how bowling fits into the modern lifestyle, and the various kinds of benefits to be expected while playing this sport.

Part 2 discusses all about the equipment and gear used in game of bowling. It has been noted that often times, players jump right in without realizing the need to understand the equipment before having to start building any skills. To know more about how to find the right bowling ball, the section; *Selecting Your Bowling Ball* has all the information and for those who have no idea what a reactive resin cover stock is, you can discover more about what cover stocks really are in *Mastering Bowling Ball Cover Stocks.*

To discover more about pin racks, and the reason behind the particular manner of behavior showed by bowling pins when hit by bowling balls, then head over to *Rack & Pins.* And finally, a special discussion on bowling shoes have also been prepared in the section *Bowling Shoes and Why They Count.*

Not only will I help you in selecting gear, I am also going to help you know how to maintain it. This is found in the section *Maintenance Tips for Bowling Balls.*

Part 3 of this book discusses the basic skills involved bowling. For an extensive discussion of proper behavior in bowling alleys, read the section *Etiquette… Or How to Bowl Like a Sir/Madame.*

If you also want to learn how to manually score a bowling game, information is provided about it in *The Scoring System in Bowling. The concept of* Proper finger grip is also discussed in *Gripping a Bowling Ball for the Fist Time.*

Part 4 of the book deals with the various advanced techniques and strategies involved in the game. To learn more about the ideal oil used in bowling lanes, head over to *Oil Patterns.* An extensive exploration of the minute adjustments needed for a better game is provided in the section *Adjustment Guidelines.*

Part 1: Introduction

It Started One Fine Day...

I started bowling when I was about seven years old. At that time, I started, I didn't think much of it – it was just one of those things that you did with your family and friends. It is a game that takes your mind off of things, and you find yourself being grateful that you have something to do in lace of homework on the weekends.

Gradually, as I grew into an adult, the game bowling slowly became more like therapy for me. Weekly therapy, I might add. Several years late, bowling became more than just a recreational activity for me. I joined several bowling clubs, and right now, I'm proud to say that I've tried at least once bowling alley in every city that I have visited.

Yes, I am your typical bowling nut. I've also made it a point to buy new bowling balls by saving some cash. For this sport, equipment is of high importance, but its importance is not comparable to acquiring the skill, which can only be acquired with continuous practice.

Bowling, as many of you may already know, is one of those things in life from your own point of view, looks really simple if you're just watching someone do it, but the very moment you are the one holding the ball, it becomes a real challenge to deal with.

Bowling, as a sport, is challenging because a play can only be perfect when you have acquired the right methods and skills. Of course, only a small percentage of bowlers end up becoming professionals in the sport. But then again, there is nothing wrong with you trying to improve your play by acquiring and applying the right knowledge and skills.

This book that you are reading now is a result of many years of experience acquired from bowling. Before I continue, I would like to clarify right away that I am not a professional. If you were expecting some pro-level guy to be your guide to bowling, unfortunately, that is not me.

However, I do assure you that the information contained within this book is the same information applied by professionals while keeping their games up. For every professional in bowling, there is a vast bank of knowledge regarding the sport. This knowledge base is termed bowling theory.

When you want to try something new, theory application is of importance. For example, if you are unable to produce any strikes during that once-weekly game with your friends, there is definitely something wrong with your approach. To correct this, you need to learn the basics and thereafter, learn the advanced methods for improving your play.

An interesting fact about bowling is that it is a very friendly and approachable sport. Truth is, it is not a super easy sport, but it is one of the few sports that gets to allow even six-year-olds to just pick up a plastic bowling ball and go.

Bowling is also one of the few sports that's very open to anyone who wishes to try it. Bowling centers and small-town bowling alleys when alone might not be the most glamorous places to be, but with your friends or family, you have the assurance that you are going to have a good time, not mindful of your score and present handicap for that week.

To a certain degree, I guess this has been one of the main reasons why most commercial bowling centers are still alive and kicking. The marketing strategies used may have changed a little over the years, but the core principles of having fun and just giving it your best shot have not changed and have remained even with the passing years.

So, whenever you head over to a bowling alley, I want you to make your number one priority -enjoyment and not winning.

I know this may seem to be a very non-competitive angle for some people who will complain, but let me clarify: when one truly loves what he/she is doing, and genuinely enjoys him- or herself, the mind shows more efficiency in storing any motor-related information. If you are having fun, your mind tends to effectively remember more of your best shots and your strongest movements.

Thus, to improve in your game subconsciously, having fun, in a sense, is really an expert's method of achieving that.

So, if you dislike what you are doing, and you are also constantly thinking that bowling is a colossal waste of time, then you will have a really tough time having to learn new methods and using them to improve your play. Also, your number one priority shouldn't be to get five strikes in a row – it is enjoyment. Relax, be yourself and most importantly, enjoy the game!

The Evolution of Bowling

Bowling is more than just pure enjoyment – it's actually a calorie-burning workout! Swinging a heavy bowling ball is just similar to lifting static weights like dumbbells and performing explosive movements with a Russian kettlebell.

The history of bowling is well-documented, and there are actually exhibits and museums scattered throughout the world that show how this sport has evolved over the years.

The concept of bowling has been estimated to using a sphere to knock down targets from over a distance and has been around for over two thousand years now.

Crude play sets found in Egypt serves as one of the earliest pieces of evidence that shows that bowling has been in the imagination of mankind for a long time. With the passing years, bowling eventually evolved into something that is more than recreation – it has become a serious sport, and the rest, as they say, is history.

Today throughout the globe, there are countless organizations that uphold its regulations and standards.

I encourage everyone, however, to overlook the fact that bowling has evolved into a professional sport. I want you guys to go bowling because you feel like bowling, and because you really want to have!

Also, bowling isn't just good for your mind and your social life; it's actually good for your body, too! Bowling as a physical activity, even from its history, can be compared to lifting dumbbells in the gym, or swinging Russian kettlebells.

If you are using heavy bowling balls that aren't completely made of plastic, your muscles and joints tend to get a great workout whenever you decide that it's time to practice your strikes with your family and friends.

Part 2: Balls & Pins

Just as seen in other sport, bowling has its own weapon of choice – the bowling ball. Then your rolling spheres target – the pins. In this section of the book, all the details related to bowling equipment will be talked about, thereafter, the various techniques and special bowling methods will be discussed.

It is of importance that you become acquainted with using the bowling gear if you really want to improve your play. Granted, it's not all about balls and pins when it comes to bowling.

However, it is important that you become aware of the various subtle differences between the different kinds of bowling balls or, for example, what to expect when you are using a plastic ball instead of a conventional bowling ball. These are the one of the many issues that may have a big impact on your play, so it's best to explore this area as well.

Selecting Your Bowling Balls

If this is your first time bowling, then of course you will want to get and use the best bowling ball. You will be surprised to know that you just can't really narrow down your selection of bowling balls based on any brand or make the choice alone.

Based on specific criteria, you have to select a bowling ball with intimate connection to your performance *while you use the ball itself.*

So, are you ready to select your first-ever bowling ball? The following are my best pieces of advice which would help you avoid buying a bowling ball that will end up not improving your game:

1. When selecting a ball, the first thing that you have to keep in mind is its weight. The normal weight for bowling balls is 16 pounds or 7.27 kilos. A majority of bowlers buy or use bowling balls that weigh this much.

   Yet, there are also a lot of bowlers who tend to use lighter balls (which are usually just a pound lighter), just because they feel that the extra pound doesn't help their game.

   How should *you* select a ball? If you are to buy your own bowling ball, I would highly recommend that you select and buy a ball that is tied with your own body weight.

   There is this old formula that still works today: multiply your body weight by ten percent and, voila – you will get the ideal ball weight.

   However, note that if you have an above-average body weight, do not consider getting a ball that weighs *more than sixteen pounds.*

   Remember this one fact: The game of bowling requires applying a lot of backswings and releasing, so if your ball is too heavy for you and you are not very adept in controlling it yet, you might end up hurting yourself.

Another technique is to add at least an extra pound (up to a maximum of two pounds) to the current weight of the bowling balls that you use in your local bowling alley.

So, if your local bowling alley has twelve-pound or thirteen-pound house balls, you can opt for either a fifteen-pounder or a sixteen-pounder. Either way, the maximum should always be sixteen pounds, because it is the recognized upper limit which is safe for average bowlers.

Another thing that you should keep in mind is the finger holes in the ball. I know that there are a lot of bowling balls out there that have been pre-drilled.

Also, I know that while shopping online or offline, one tends to usually look out for the best and most convenient deal of all.

Is a pre-drilled bowling ball a good investment? Not if you ask someone who has been using custom-drilled balls all his life.

This is not really a question of vanity; it's more of a question about using a bowling ball with finger holes which are actually the shape and size of your own fingers.

Think about it this way: the "life" of your swings depends on ball control. Ball control, on the other hand, depends on how well you are able to hold on to your ball.

If you have to squeeze your fingers in because your fingers don't really fit into the bowling ball, every time you throw a ball, you will be half-distracted.

Have you ever seen someone who has naturally thick fingers throw a regular house ball? On close observation, as he releases the ball, an additional amount of effort is put in as it is needed in order to control the ball when thrown into the lane.

This extra effort is needed because either the bowler's fingers are partially stuck (due to having to force the digits in) or they are not sufficiently *in* the finger holes at all.

To avoid all these hassles, you need to have your new bowling ball custom-drilled. It's not that expensive, and remember this: it's not every day that you buy a killer bowling ball right?

2. Another factor to consider is the bowling ball's cover stock. There are different kinds of cover stocks, like your regular plastic cover stock and reactive resin. We will later on, discuss the key differences between the various commonly used cover stocks for bowling balls.

Because each cover stock has its own set of benefits and disadvantages, it's important that you choose wisely depending on your need for the game and how well the peculiar tendencies of different cover stocks can be managed by you.

3. The third step is actually going out and selecting your new bowling ball.

   Nothing beats the experience of going to a physical pro store to select your new killer bowling ball. You get to see and hold the different kinds of bowling balls, *plus* you can ask for discounts from the store owner or staff (whenever it's possible, discounts *are* given by some stores).

   You can always shop online, if you do not have the luxury of time to drive to a pro store. However, I highly recommend that your choice of an online pro store would be one that has a custom drilling service. Custom drilling is *not free* in most cases.

   The usual drilling fee is about $30, but the final fee tends to really depend on a lot of factors, such as how big the holes have to be, and what kind of ball you want.

   Suffice to say, but it's rare for a drilling service to go over $100, but again, it all depends on the store's pricing and the kind of labor and machinery to be used to get the job done.

   What about the price of the bowling ball itself? If you are on a tight budget *and* still want your bowling ball to be custom-drilled in order to fit your fingers correctly, I would say you would have to spend *at least* $100 for a new ball inclusive of the drilling service. Lots of pro stores run their sales at least once a month, so you can expect a good deal to pop up pretty soon.

The more popular brands are priced at about $150 to $200 per ball. Other commercial brands, geared towards beginners, can cost anywhere from $45 to $75. With regards to weight availability (as it can also affect cost in some cases), most brands tend to offer 1 pound increments starting from 10 pounds.

4. Let's discuss custom-drilling a little more, because some of you may have some questions that have not been addressed completely in the previous item.

   The most common question people ask when I get to talk to them about custom-drilling new bowling balls is "why is it *really* necessary?" I actually have several reasons for recommending it.

   First of all, using a custom-drilled bowling ball really helps to improve your game, as it grants better grip and, consequently, gives you better ball control.

   While gripping a bowling ball with your fingers, your hand muscles will work overtime in order to control the speed and power of the ball. So, if your fingers can't grip the ball properly, you *will have poor* control over it.

   Remember, a bowling ball is really just interested in two things: rolling and falling. If you can't control a sixteen-pound ball that is smooth all over, you run the risk of crushing either your toes, or someone else's foot. And this brings us to another important reason why custom-drilling is necessary: safety.

In order to minimize the risk of over-straining your shoulders and consequently crushing your unsuspecting toes, then get a custom-drilled ball. It is a little difficult to describe how it feels while you are holding a custom-drilled ball.

The best description I can give you is that you will feel *lighter* by a few pounds compared to house balls or any other ball that doesn't really fit your fingers well. When something feels lighter, it becomes easier to manipulate and throw around, right?

5. When you have finally acquired your new custom-drilled ball, I would implore you to *give yourself time* to get used to it. People who have never used a custom bowling ball usually assume that they will have the same experience as they had while using house balls.

This isn't true, because now you have a ball that actually fits your fingers' physical dimensions! Give yourself one or two whole games to get used to your new custom ball if you have become so accustomed to house balls that barely complement your fingers. Trust me; when you finally master how to handle it, you will *love* your new weapon of choice!

Mastering Bowling Ball Cover Stocks

In the previous section as I have already discussed, there are four different kinds of cover stocks used for bowling balls. The pros and cons of each type will be discussed here, as well as some expert tips to follow while handling each type of cover stock.

The important thing to note here is that your choice of a cover stock should be made based on what complements your strength as a bowler. For example, you probably would work better with regular polyester/plastic cover stock, if you always throw the ball in such a way that it travels a really straight line, then.

A lot of bowling centers and bowling alleys purchase house balls that have polyester cover stocks because they are great for beginners, and such bowling balls were designed to travel as straight a line as possible.

The various pros and cons of four different kinds of cover stocks commonly used on commercial bowling balls includes.

Polyester Bowling Balls

Because Polyester or plastic bowling balls actually repel the oil that coats the lanes, they are highly recommended for beginners. Yes, bowling lanes actually have *oil* on them, so don't be surprised if its flooring feels slippery.

Pros:

- The most common kind of cover stock used in bowling centers and bowling alleys around the world

- Easy to find and acquire from online and offline pro stores

- Repels oil

- Comes in light and easy-to-manage weights

- Primarily designed to travel a distinctly straight line regardless of the intended direction of the bowler

- Excellent for targeting spares

- Serves as an excellent choice for recreational players who just want to enjoy the game a few times per month

- It's cheaper when compared to other cover stocks

- Can be custom-drilled to fit your fingers perfectly

- Definitely a better alternative to the older, and less manageable, house balls that have seen better days

- Low cost way to get started with serious bowling

Cons

- Because of their inherent limitations (e.g. tendency to stick to a straight path), Polyester balls are rarely used as strike balls

- For intermediate bowlers who want to improve their game by trying other techniques and throwing patterns, it is not the best ball.

- It is not recommended for those who want to practice hooks, which is commonly used for strikes

Urethane Bowling Balls

To level up your game, you can transition smoothly from plastic bowling balls to urethane bowling balls. People who want to try other bowling techniques are often recommended Urethane balls.

Pros:
- Oil-repelling

- Popular with intermediate to advanced players

- A must-have for your bowling arsenal

- Excellent for dry bowling lanes

- Excellent option for a novice bowler who wishes to start on bowling hooks

- Can be easily polished to suit the owner's particular needs

- Can travel a consistent direct or curved path each and every time

- Bowlers can pick up their urethane balls when they are unable to perform consistently with other balls.

Cons:

- Sometime, it can be too consistent (e.g. it continues travelling the same path, even if you want to deviate a little to target specific pins)

- Not the best ball if from an angle, you want to hit pins

- Not the ideal ball for continuous strikes

Reactive Resin Bowling Balls

Bowling ball manufacturers started using resin particles when they started tinkering with the idea of a stronger gripping power for balls. Urethane and resin actually cover reactive resin bowling balls.

The idea behind reactive resin balls is actually quite simple: you have a ball that will just explode when it reaches the dry part of the bowling lane when you increase the friction potential of the ball, even on passing through the oil part.

If this sounds interesting to you, here are the pros and cons of the reactive resin cover stock:

Pros:

- Powerful backend for killer hooks

- Creates more friction if the bowling center uses common house oil patterns

- Increases your chances of throwing strikes

- More ideal for throws intended to hit the pins at an angle

- Recommended for advanced bowlers who want a more complete arsenal.

Cons

- Not the best option for bringing down spares or the random pin/s that do not go down on the first throw
- High tendency to hook means you will also have to put in extra effort to throw straight balls
- Generally pricier than urethane balls and plastic balls.

Rack & Pins

On bowling for the first time, you have to take into consideration four main things: the bowling ball, the lane, the pin rack, and the pins.

These make up the main components needed for a good bowling game. In this part of the book, the bowling pins and the design of the pin rack are going to be discussed, so you will understand how these components behave, and the reason behind this particular design.

Let's talk about the bowling pins first. Bowling pins rarely get any limelight because no one is really interested in holding one, and generally, people don't get to see them up close. Bowlers are usually concerned with just one thing – hammering down all the pins with a victorious strike!

While it is true that a lot of people master bowling without ever knowing what the bowling pins are like in the first place, it's still better that you have this knowledge, because it provides with a better understanding as to why the pins behave the way they do when rammed down by a rolling sphere.

In centers and alleys, the standard bowling pins used are actually made of *wood.* Yes, I know this might come as a surprise to many of you, since they look like they're made of hard plastic. Bowling pins are not actually completely made of plastic.

The plastic that you are actually seeing is just the outer cover, or outer layer, of the bowling pin. It serves as a protection for the wood inside while reducing the friction between the pins when they fall.

The height of a standard bowling pin is always fifteen inches, although I am sure you must have seen smaller bowling pins, especially in special alleys that feature different variations of duckpin bowling.

Duckpin bowling pins are stouter and shorter than your regular ten-pin bowling pin. With regards to the weight, standard 10-pin bowling pins will weigh no less than 3 pounds per pin.

On continuous play, bowling pins, like other sports equipment, are eventually worn down. Any bowling center operator worth his name will have at least two sets of bowling pins.

The bowling center operator will elect to change the bowling pins, midway through peak bowling season in order to give the first pin set of the season a break. When done this way, bowling pins that are given at least one break per season will definitely last longer than pins continuously used.

Rotation of pins is essential to keep up the quality of your games. If you are throwing really well, and the pins end up not behaving quite like they used to, it is possible that they have already become too worn out.

Rather than feeling frustrated with yourself, simply ask the staff or the owner how much play-time the pins have gotten in the season. If the staff or owner says that the pins have not been rotated yet, then it is possible that the pins are the cause of your less-than ideal scores.

In such cases, just keep playing! Don't let the pin condition deter you from practicing your hooks and strikes. Just keep in mind that your throws may not produce the best results you desire, because the pins themselves are already worn out from having weathered too many games at that season.

Now that we're done discussing the bowling pins, let's move on to the pin rack and the pin deck. Some people use these two terms interchangeably and there's really no harm in doing that. However, it is important that I clarify that the pin rack is not the same thing as the pin deck.

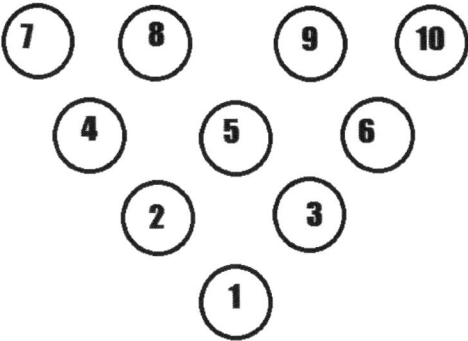

The equilateral orientation of bowling pins in a standard pin rack. A corresponding number assigned for each pin helps identify which area needs to be targeted in the next throw.

The pin rack is comprised of the actual bowling pins in their familiar triangular orientation.

So, you have ten equally-sized bowling pins that are of uniform distance from each other. The pin deck, on the other hand, actually refers to the space accommodating the bowling pins.

Let's talk about the standard distances used in a pin rack. From a player's usual starting position, it seems as if the bowling pins are really close together.

But in reality, bowling pins standing in a standard pin rack are twelve inches away from each other. For pins that are aligned with each other like pins 3 and 9, the total distance is 20.75 inches.

The distance between the first pin and the last pin on either side of the triangular orientation is exactly 36 inches. From these measurements, as you can see, a very precise system is used in determining how far apart each pin will be from other pins in the rack.

This is the reason why bowling alleys need to invest in the use of special machines that produce an accurate pin rack after every strike or spare.

There are certain standards that have to be maintained, even during recreational games, and the only way that these standards can be appropriately maintained is through mechanical intervention.

Bowling Shoes and Why They Count

Bowling shoes are never a luxury if you want to bowl safely and effectively. You can do without a pair of pants, but you just can't do without a good pair of bowling shoes!

In the world of bowling, it may appear that half the time, players are more concerned with outdoing each other through buying fancy balls and bowling shoes. To a non-player it seems that way, and I certainly cannot deny that *some* players invest in pricey gear to show off.

However, it is important to understand that whenever you are playing any sport, the quality of your gear and equipment is partly dependent on your performance.

You don't need to buy too many things in bowling to get started. In as much, there are some things that you simply cannot do without – like bowling shoes.

A lot of people assume that bowling shoes (especially the ones that are for rent in bowling alleys and bowling centers) are at least mildly undesirable, given that they have been used repeatedly by other people and, quite frankly, they aren't really the best-looking pairs of shoes in the city.

Regardless of the public's general viewpoint of these bowling shoes, regardless of age and experience, bowling centers continue to insist that all players, wear them if they wish to use the facilities.

But why do bowling centers insist on such a strange policy? Are bowling centers soulless commercial centers bent on vacuuming every spare dollar from unsuspecting bowlers?

The answer is: not really. While it is undeniable that some commercial bowling centers can be a little too insistent that you spend more than what you have allotted for your bowling night, I still can't say that using bowling shoes are luxurious or unnecessary.

These shoes are actually designed to work with the kind of surface normally found in bowling lanes. A good pair of bowling shoes can spell the difference between a powerful hook, and a gutter ball. Your actual delivery is influenced by your choice of footwear when you bowl, or during the release, of the bowling ball.

Let's try to break down what happens when you release a bowling ball, to see how a pair of flat, colorful shoes will fit into this scenario. The first step is to grab your bowling ball right? What's the next step? You go near the lane and you then perform your backswing.

The backswing is an extremely powerful component of the delivery, because you will need to balance your body and aim the ball well at the same time.

In order to maintain your balance during the delivery, your feet have to be agile, with the floor cooperating with your movements.

Otherwise, you will end up stumbling, and even dropping, the bowling ball.

With your bowling shoes, you will perform these chain of movements, even if the *approach* or the space before the foul line has something that might prevent you from performing a successful throw or delivery (e.g. a sticky, chewed-up piece of gum from somebody else's shoe).

Also, the use of your bowling shoes helps to keep the bowling center clean. Successful delivery or throwing is dependent on a whole lot of factors, including the cleanliness of the premises' floors. If everyone could walk into the bowling alley with their regular street shoes, trust me, you will be playing in a less ideal environment.

Always keep your bowling shoes clean, if you have own, and avoid using them anywhere else other than the play area. If you have to go outside to the car or have to visit the bathroom, take them off. Dry, dirt-free bowling shoes are a boon to everyone.

Maintenance Tips for Bowling Balls

Given that your bowling ball is your main gear whenever you go out to bowl, it is essential that you maintain your bowling balls regularly by polishing them. With regards to maintaining any kind bowling ball, here are some things to keep in mind:

1. You definitely have to clean your bowling balls, if they have gone through twelve games. At your some spare time, after every *sixth game,* clean and polish your bowling balls so as to keep them in top condition.

   The skills of the bowler are complemented by well-maintained balls and, in bowling, when your gear is well-maintained, your skills can only then be expressed effectively.

2. Wet or well-oiled lanes can make your balls more slippery. Slippery balls often lose their tendency to hook or curve when they grip the dry part of the lane.

   On the other hand, balls extensively used in relatively dry conditions will hook more than they should, because of excess friction they encounter whenever you play with it. Either way, cleaning and polishing will help sort out any problems after extensive play.

3. If you really want to improve your play, and also more than willing to put in the extra time and effort to keep your gear pristine, then you have to clean and polish all the bowling balls you frequently use after every series.

A series is simply three bowling games in a row. Usually people polish their bowling balls after every sixth game, but when in the mood for better games and a consistently diminishing handicap, cleaning after every *series* is definitely a worthy option to take.

Part 3: Play It Right

In the history of man, every sport has its own set of standards and rules. These rules are sometimes viewed as limiting, but then again, they have been around for a long time in order to keep the sports stable and playable.

We may not always like the laid down rules and the best practices, but continuous play of the sport will make you realize that whoever made the rules sure knew what he was doing! In this part of the book, some of the basics of bowling like etiquette and scoring.

There is no harm in reviewing some of the subsections just to refresh your memory if you already have this knowledge. But if you don't really know how this game works yet, then I would recommend that you read this section at least twice, to avail you the opportunity of having a better feel of the sport itself.

But then again, the most important thing is to still have fun and enjoy yourself when you go out bowling. So, my suggestion is that you learn these guidelines by heart, and try to apply them as frequently as possible so they won't be a bother when you try to remember.

Etiquette... Or How to Bowl Like a Sir/Madame

Because I wanted to emphasize the need for players to practice some common courtesies when they are playing, I purposefully created a funny title for this subsection.

Even though it is completely fine to enjoy your bowling night with your friends, it is also equally important to ensure that for *others* who also want to enjoy their night out with friends and family, you are not making the night hard.

Here are some etiquette guidelines that are applicable for most bowling alleys and similar recreational centers that offer bowling:

1. Before stepping into the playing area, look at your feet. Are you putting on bowling shoes? If you are, go ahead! If not, *stop* and go back to the front desk, and ask to rent a pair for yourself and anyone else in your group who doesn't have them.

    Wearing a pair of bowling shoes *is* a form of courtesy in the bowling alley. If you feel that the rentable shoes in your bowling alley are horrendous, then just get a pair for yourself.

    Just make sure that you don't use your bowling shoes anywhere else. As soon as you are done bowling, and ready to step back to the street and drive home, take off your bowling shoes and put them in a shoe carrier. Shoe carriers are cheap!

    You can actually buy one (or two) from eBay at a couple of bucks each. The idea is this: when you wear bowling shoes, whenever you play, you are sending a message to everyone else in the bowling alley.

You are communicating to them that you want to keep the premises clean and free of dirt and every other icky stuff that might end up impeding on a person's movement when he is about to deliver a ball.

What if you see people in the bowling alley who are wearing street sneakers?

Well, it would be best not to confront them directly about their shoes. What you can safely do if the situation is really bothering you is to talk to the person in charge so *he* can tell the other group to take off their street shoes.

Being a smart bowler, partly involves knowing when *not* to interfere with the proceedings of a bowling alley. Leave that to the "professionals" – which is mainly just the staff in charge.

2. Watch your language when you are playing in any bowling center or bowling alley.

   I know that it is very easy to lose yourself in a game; after all, you are playing because you are very passionate about the sport, and a lot of time, effort and money is been invested into it in order for you to become really good at it.

   However, this still does not entitle you to use foul language or curse words during the course of playing the game. Sure, your closest buddies might find it really funny. And maybe they feel more at home if they hear someone's outbursts every now and then.

But, the hard truth of the matter is that other people are there with you on the premises and, *other people* don't appreciate such outbursts, regardless of what you might be feeling at the moment.

So, whenever you feel like cursing because your hook shot didn't go as planned, let others enjoy their game and just hold in your feeling.

3. Bowling lanes were meant to be as pristine and clean as possible. Unfortunately, some people forget that they have to keep the premises clean when they play.

I'm not quick to judge, but from years of experience I have come to the conclusion that any player who brings a big soda or other food items near the bowling lanes is generally bad news.

The risk of injury increases, when beverages or food are spilled on or around the lanes, because the floor area near the actual lanes needs to be free of visible contaminants.

For example, if someone spills a small quantity of soda on the approach area, as that soda dries, it can become sticky.

A sticky approach area can cause someone to momentarily lose balance during a delivery. The result? Well, let's just say the outcome of such a scenario is rarely desirable.

So, keep your food and beverages as far away as possible from the lanes, for your own safety and the safety of others.

Despite all of these, if you want to really improve your game, all you really need to bring to the lanes are your best bowling balls and your killer techniques!

4. Since, bowlers are generally an impatient bunch of people, always be ready to take your turn whenever you are playing with six or more people and at the same time you are using only one or two lanes for some reason.

   Not only is this polite, but it will also help speed up the game and avoid ruining the fun of others. Spending time with friends is quite nice, but when you end up forcing others to wait too long, no one is going to have a lot of fun.

5. The foul line is present in the arena for a reason: it helps to refine your delivery *and to* also keep others safe. How so? Well, as I have touched upon that earlier in this book, bowling lanes actually have two regions: a wet region and a dry region.

   The wet region is usually coated with house oil. This oil helps to reduce friction and as well help sustain the speed and power of a delivered bowling ball.

   The foul line serves as a clear separation between the approach (which is another dry region) and the wet region wherein the house oil has been coated. So, whenever you step over the foul line you are essentially getting a small quantity of oil on your bowling shoes.

If you keep stepping over the foul line, a little gradually becomes *a lot* and you will be spreading small patches of oil all over the approach.

Not only will you end up endangering yourself because of the misplaced oil, you also endanger *others* who are playing on the same lane as you. So, to be safe and to keep others safe, just follow this particular rule and avoid stepping over the foul line at all costs.

6. it is customary for each player to ignore all the other balls *except* his own bowling balls, when balls are rolled back to the starting point of the lane. Use house balls instead if you don't have a bowling ball of your own.

And, while it is tempting to practice your hook shot with another person's new bowling ball with some new hybrid urethane cover stock, it is against common bowling courtesy to do that.

If you want to borrow a fellow player's bowling ball, ask permission first. Remember – some bowling balls cost over $200 or $300 each.

A player who has an expensive bowling ball will of course be protective of his investment. If you are jealous that everyone else has a special set of bowling balls, then why not try investing in your own. Until that time when you would have your own gear, stick to the house balls.

7. The area behind the foul line (a.k.a. the approach) is sacred ground for bowlers.

   When someone else is playing, *don't* stand on the approach or anywhere near it. If you are excited that someone is going to be throwing another killer strike, stand a few feet away from the person.

   Behind the person is the most ideal position if you really want to observe another person's technique. Your presence is a very unwelcome distraction when you stand anywhere near the player.

   A person's normal line of sight is actually quite wide, so even if your intention is not to distract the current bowler, your position (e.g. where you are standing) might be cutting into the bowler's line of sight.

8. If there is another player on the lane that is right beside *your lane,* don't do anything that will distract or disrupt the other player. Also, do try to avoid throwing your ball into the adjacent lane.

   It is very frustrating to suddenly see a wayward ball intruding upon your own lane.

   How would you feel if someone else accidentally threw his ball into your own lane? I'm sure you wouldn't pick a fight, but that you wouldn't feel completely okay, I'm sure.

The Scoring System in Bowling

Many bowling alleys in the United States and elsewhere have automatic systems for scoring. In order to improve the overall enjoyment of players, bowling centers have invested in special computers that do all the scoring for you.

However, if you are a serious player it doesn't hurt to actually understand how your scores are being tallied. The theory is important, because integrally, the scoring system and the actual game are tied together.

You can create goals for yourself if you knew how a perfect score is achieved per game so you can gradually improve your overall handling of the game over time.

Gradual improvement over a period of weeks or even months is awesome, because once you have finally mastered a particular skill; the skill tends to stay with you forever.

So, let's discuss the basics of the scoring system for bowling. In a regular ten-pin bowling game, it consists of ten frames, or basically ten chances for you to get a strike or at least a spare. Here are the scoring rules:

1. While playing a game of bowling, your maximum possible score is three hundred. The minimum possible score is zero (no negatives, so even if it's not your day, your lowest possible score in bowling is just naught).

   Your score in bowling is dependent on how many pins you knock down during a throw or delivery. "Delivery" and "throwing" are equivalent to "shots" or "shooting" in basketball. Use the right lingo to really get into the game!

2. When you throw a ball and it demolishes all ten pins that is called a *strike.* A perfect shot (all ten pins down) is distinguished on the score sheet by a big **X** mark.

   If you make a delivery and a few pins remain standing, you will have a chance to knock those down with a second throw. When you knock down all the remaining pins on the second throw that is called a spare. A spare is denoted by a **/** (slash) on the score sheet.

   So, remember this: a strike (**X**) is a perfect throw that knocks down all ten pins, and if it takes two throws to knock down all ten pins that is a spare (**/**). Don't confuse the two, and definitely try to avoid making a mistake if you are in charge of the score sheet on any bowling night!

3. Ten frames are seen in a game of bowling and each frame gives each player a maximum of two throws or *rolls.*

   When you throw a strike on the first roll, your score is a ten, plus the score of the remaining roll.

4. What if you don't score a strike on your first roll? That's okay. If you knock down six pins on your first throw, your score would be a worthy *six.* So, let's say on the first roll you got a six, followed by an eight.

   Your total score for that frame will be 6 + 8 = 14. The perfect score for each frame is always 30, and this is only possible if you knocked down 10 pins for each roll because each frame allows a maximum of two rolls, or chances, only.

5. The equivalent score on a spare is 10. Unless you throw a ball for the second frame, you would not have a total score yet. So, let's say you scored 10 on the first frame because of a spare. Throwing a seven on the first throw of the second frame makes your total score to be 17.

   For a frame, the highest possible score where a spare occurs is 20 and can only be achieved if you threw a spare followed by a victorious strike. Both spares and strikes are equivalent to 10, so the equivalent score if you add a spare and a strike is 20.

6. When a player does not throw a strike or a spare, the total score is gotten from just the number of pins that are knocked down. In the occasion when a spare or strike does not occur, the current frame is categorized as an "open frame."

   So, let's say on your first throw, you knocked down six pins, and on your next throw you knocked down another two pins. At this point, a spare cannot be announced, because two more pins are still standing, so the total score will only be eight for that frame.

Gripping a Bowling Ball for the First Time

It's time to move on to the basic techniques that will allow anyone to develop their bowling skills at an accelerated pace now that we are done discussing etiquette and the scoring system in bowling. Some of you might be wondering: what is the essence of reviewing the basics?

Well, every sport has its own set of basic skills, and if lack mastery over these basic skills, I would be difficult progressing to the more advanced techniques of the sport.

Skills involved in sporting are interconnected. Learning how to bowl well can be likened to building a house. You lay down the foundations first, and you have to make sure that you are not building your new house on soft, sinking ground.

As soon as the foundation is set, you can start adding the floors, walls, and the ceilings. Once the house is finally complete, you can then begin furnishing it. The furnishing part is the refinement process seen in bowling.

Refinement can be achieved by acquiring advanced techniques, and continuous practice of these new techniques as often as possible. Later on in the book, we will be covering very specific techniques.

Now, a good bowler always has the proper gear, knowledge, and most of all, an *effective ball grip*. Gripping a heavy bowling ball requires proper form, and it's an art on its own. So, let's get started:

1. Look at your bowling ball, and find the finger holes. For standard ten-pin bowling, a conventional bowling ball has three finger holes. There are two medium-sized

finger holes on top, and a much larger finger hole just directly beneath the two.

The thumb grips the biggest finger hole, while the two smaller finger holes were designed to be able to accommodate the middle finger (that's the first hole) and the ring finger (second hole).

2. Next, slide your fingers into the ball's holes. The two fingers on top should go *halfway* in, while your thumb should go *all* the way in. To give additional support and to control the ball, your index finger and pinkie should be spread out a little.

The strain of carrying a heavy bowling ball should be offset by your hand, wrist, and arm. Simply put, do not allow your *fingers* to do all the lifting! If you do this, you increase the risk of injuring your hand during a vicious throw.

There should be a concerted effort between fingers, hand, and whole arm. During the backswing, it is easy to just let the fingers do the work. However, our fingers were not created to *carry* weight. They were designed for gripping, leaving your arms and legs to do all the lifting.

So, when you grip a standard bowling ball, make sure that your thumb is doing most of the stabilizing work, because it was designed for carrying out such extensive manipulation.

The thumb is the strongest digit on the human hand; that's why it's bigger, and it's positioned that way on your hand.

The two fingers atop are mainly there for aiming and guiding the ball during the course of its release, while the other two fingers that are outside also help guide the ball during its delivery.

Throwing Hooks

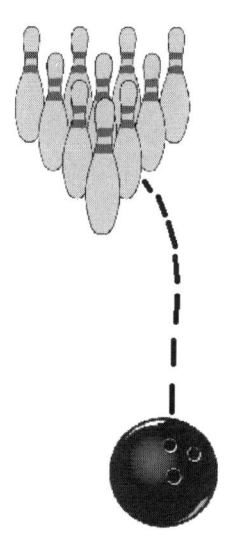

The basic trajectory of a hook shot

Earlier in this book I mentioned the importance of throwing hooks if you want to pick up spares. In this part, I'm going to make sure that you learn how to easily knock down those random pins that did not collapse when you first rolled out your bowling ball.

1. In the previous section, I mentioned that the cover stock of your bowling ball has an influence on how easily you will be able to throw a hook.

Ideally, to facilitate hooks, you should use a bowling ball with a reactive resin cover stock. Is it possible to throw hooks even while using a regular, plastic house ball?

Yes. In all reality, people throw hooks all the time in bowling alleys, and they don't realize that they are using old house balls with polyester cover stock. Accidentally, it is fairly easy to hook a shot. However, to produce a calculated and well-aimed hook, it becomes more difficult.

Under two conditions a ball can hook either because of dry lane conditions or just because the ball hasn't been polished sufficiently after a few games. Despite these conditions, if you want to throw well-calculated hooks to knock down those spares, you need a ball with the right cover stock to achieve that (e.g. reactive resin).

Also, a custom-drilled bowling ball is not needed to learn how to throw hooks.

So, don't use this as a compelling reason not to study hooking a ball, because it's a really lousy reason. Let me repeat: people hook their bowling balls all the time! All you need to do is to learn how to hook a bowling ball when you *really need to.*

2. Hooking a bowling ball doesn't require any fancy or trained footwork; simply, approach the foul line as you would any time.

    Within the arm movement, lies the secret of throwing an effective hook. Some bowlers like to throw the ball in such a way that their arm crosses their chest area a little in the process of the final release.

When the ball is released, the arm swings up in the general direction of the shoulder.

Does this actually work? Well, if you want to impress your novice friends, it doesn't hurt to use this as your style. But quite honestly, it does not really add anything beneficial to the hooking of the ball.

I would recommend that you keep your arm as straight as possible during the backswing and the actual forward swing. Think of your throwing arm as a massive pendulum.

The weight at the end of the pendulum is the bowling ball, and your body is just follows the logical result of swinging a weight with a straight and firm arm. Another important factor to remember is the speed of the ball.

Do not add extra force to your downswing by trying to enhance the bowling ball's acceleration. Allow gravity to do what it does best – let it pull your arm down as you feel the weight being magnetically attracted to the bowling lane.

When you are attempting to throw a well-aimed hook, some people insist that adding a little more force to your throw will improve your chances of success. In reality, applying an additional force during the downswing and release is way much harder to control.

Using excess force increases the tendency for the bowling ball to overshoot once it finally grips the dry part of the lane.

The result? A painful gutter ball. So, rather than trying to outdo gravity's constant downward pull, focus on the sensation of a natural hook, so it can become a second nature to you.

With regards to the actual release, there are several steps that you should keep in mind:

- Aim the ball well, and maintain your eye on the target. Delivery or release in the game of bowling is similar to shooting a rifle or pistol. Don't lower your shooting/throwing hand until just after the bowling ball is rapidly rolling toward the pins. This is what is called the follow through.

- During the release of a hook, your hand should be slightly above chest level. Imagine it as having to suddenly shake someone's hand after releasing a ball.

  It sounds funny, but this is an extremely effective visualization. Don't try to cross your arm across your chest.

  It doesn't help, and frankly, switching rapidly to the other side will strain your shoulder. If you plan to bowl for a long time in the alley/center or in the future, take care of your wrist, arm, and shoulders. Do not overwork or overstrain them.

There is a dangerous misconception while hooking a ball that has been around for a long time with regards to the wrist's participation. Many people believe that flexing your wrist, and having to use it as the main pivot for the bowling ball, is the best way to go.

Despite the fact that moving around a heavy sphere with your wrist looks impressive, it can be extremely harmful to the delicate cartilage that helps keep your hand mobile and flexible.

The best players in the bowling league avoid having to overuse their wrists, because once the wrist goes, strikes and hooks become doubly difficult to accomplish.

Throwing Accurate Straight Shots

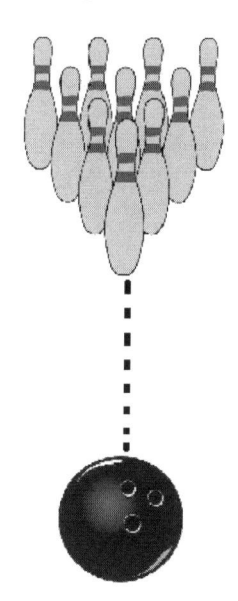

Regardless of the direction that a bowling ball is coming from, a straight shot will always produce a very linear trajectory for the released bowling ball.

The straight throw, or straight shot, is a staple of this sport. Hook shots are pretty nice, but in order to be an effective player you also need to have a good foundation in the conventional straight shot.

The straight shot is the most basic of throws, but it is also a barometer of your general expertise in bowling. Many aspiring players dismiss the straight shot as the recourse of the novice, and many bowlers forget to develop their skills at straight shots.

This is a grave mistake, because no matter how good you are with throwing hook shots, a hook shot is still different from a straight shot. You cannot substitute a straight shot for a hook shot and vice versa.

When you are bowling, these two throws have different functions and benefits. Using a straight shot, you can really power up your throw to wipe down almost all if not all of the pins on the rack.

Hook shots, on the other hand, are mainly used to pick up spares and to ram down any complicated, curved orientations on the rack. If you really want to become really good at this sport, you have to master both kinds of throws.

The following are some guidelines to ensure that your throws will ring straight and true regardless of what kind of bowling ball you happen to have:

1. The first step in throwing powerful and accurate straight shots is positioning your wrist properly. Our arms are in the same orientation as our palms which naturally point toward our pelvic area.

   You have to continuously practice rotating your wrist so that it is ready to aim and release a bowling ball in a straight manner. *Flexing* it and rotating your wrist properly are different from each other. Rotation of your wrist is painless, because your forearm tends to rotate along with it.

   Flexion, on the other hand, sets to increase your risk of injury because the wrist wasn't meant to flex as a result of having *to carry a large amount of weight*. Our wrists actually flex to allow our hands to perform fine hand movements such as writing, painting and manipulation of small objects.

   Flexing the wrist to write something is *very much different form* flexing it to carry a fifteen/sixteen pound plastic bowling ball. So again, *don't* tempt fate, and don't try to test the limits of the wrist on your throwing arm.

2. Hold the bowling ball firmly in your hand, and make your aim. When you determine where you want your bowling ball to go, swing back your arm and, while doing so, straighten your arm. Doing so would make your wrist to also straighten as your hand trails behind you during the backswing.

On reaching the natural limit of your backswing, gently rotate your wrist so that your hand and forearm will end up facing the desired direction.

As a general rule, right-handed players must have to rotate their wrists in a clockwise motion while Left-handed players must make a counter-clockwise motion prior to releasing the bowling ball.

3. Now, swing your arm forward, and let the ball naturally accelerate itself. For a straight shot, release the bowling ball just before your hand goes past your ankles. *At this level*, the actual release should also be done.

At knee or waist level, don't release the bowling ball! Releasing a sixteen pound bowling ball from knee or waist level is just plain wrong and you easily can at the end, damage wooden lanes.

And another thing: the resulting crash is really embarrassing, and other bowlers will definitely check out what's causing the ruckus! Joking aside, it is important to always release the bowling ball at the correct height.

If you have ever seen a person who released a bowling ball too late, you will know just how scary it can be for a bowling to just crash on the floor.

Releasing the bowling ball at knee level or heaven forbid, waist level, skyrockets your risk of dropping the ball accidentally on your foot, or someone else's bowling shoes.

4. The way you position your wrist and hand just before releasing the ball is the secret of a powerful straight shot.

   There should be no flexion at all; try to keep your wrist and hand as straight as a board, and then simply release the bowling ball with all the accumulated force from the backswing.

   The purpose of the backswing is to really accumulate energy in order that it builds well just before you can release the bowling ball. The backswing is like pulling the trigger of a gun: it puts together all that energy needed for a strike.

5. As I have mentioned before, never forget the follow through principle when you are bowling. For every sport that requires the propulsion of an object to a certain distance, this guiding principle should be used as it ensures that you will hit your target.

   Here's another secret of a good follow through. While performing the backswing, take a deep breath (using your nostrils) and soon as you build that momentum, breathe out and continue breathing out until your ball is rolling steadily on the lane. With a continuous exhalation, propel the ball to its intended target.

Quick Points: The Essentials of Bowling

At this point in time, I hope you have learned a lot already, and you are ready to begin studying more advanced lessons in bowling.

But before heading over to more advanced lessons, let us do a quick recap of the most important points about bowling that we have already touched upon in the previous sections of this book:

- A bowling ball can only be as good as the player who throws it. So, remove the notion that if you use an expensive bowling ball alone, your game will improve.

Getting a reliable gear is important but more importantly, you need to practice a lot, and also have fun in the process to make it easier for the mind and the body to implement new motor skills.

Bowling isn't just a purely physical sport. It requires accurate timing, fine movement, and a whole lot of mental calculation. You need to develop on your own a set of unique bowling strategies. No one can teach you those.

No one can teach you how to calm your nerves before a throw. No one else can show you how to really grip your custom-drilled ball. All of those things are acquired through learning as you continue playing the sport.

That kind of information when acquired is invaluable, and once you have it, hold on to it and build upon it because this information will be the cornerstone of every other experiences you will have when you play this sport.

- Consistency is important to bowling. Once you figure out that spot on the approach that works out for you, stick to that general area, and use it so you can get a strike every time you walk up to that spot to take a shot.

Get a feel for the lane and how it behaves, too. Within your mind, as you observe your surroundings during a bowling night, every bit of information that is processed will help increase your effectiveness as a bowler.

- If you have ever watched a pro bowler play, you will notice that his footwork is strategic. Professionals in bowling don't just walk up to the foul line and throw. Every of their movement and gesture is properly *timed* to in order that they can produce consistent results.

So, when you are moving up the foul line, make sure that whenever as you take a step, your arm is also preparing to release the ball. Imagine that you are performing a fixed set of movements prior to the release of the ball. Think like a pro, and you will get pro-level results, too.

If you at this point you are still confused, just watch any pro bowler on YouTube or on a sports channel. Watch how the legs match the backswing, downswing, and release.

These movements are not just random at all! Each pro bowler has a special peculiar style when it comes to throwing or delivering a ball, but what is certain is that they all have a system and they continually refine this system whenever possible.

- The accuracy of every throw is a result from the combination of the proper positioning of your hand and the rotation of your forearm and wrist.

Try practicing the right kind of wrist rotation for every shot. It might sound boring to do the same thing over and over again, but this is how the pros in bowling do it. You need to master each and every of these simple methods before you can learn more advanced techniques.

- It never actually hurts to think of a real strategy when you are playing. Some players think that in order to win at bowling you have to "feel it" and not "think it."

There is some grain of truth in this – you have to really let your natural instincts take over when you are playing. You must never be distracted by the details or the events happening by the side.

However, this does not mean that strategizing is completely out of the picture. Strategizing prior to a game, or during a game, is important if you want to adapt to house ball quality, lane conditions, etc.

- Three main factors influence the effectiveness of your shots. The first one is the speed of the ball which is determined by lane conditions, the quality of the throw, and the kind of ball you are using.

The second factor involved is *angles.* You must learn how to throw a ball *at an angle* so that it enters the pin deck, so you end up hitting those really difficult pins that have evaded your bowling ball thus far. The third main factor is strength.

How strongly will your bowling ball hit the pins? You can have a higher influence on the power factor of your bowling ball by ensuring that your wrist and hand are properly positioned prior to release.

Part 4: Play It Smart

Now that we are done with basic strategies of bowling, it's time to learn some advanced lessons and techniques which would really bring your skills up to pro level.

Oil Patterns

First off, let's start off this section with a discussion of *oil patterns.* If you have been with me all the way since the beginning of the book you probably would figure out already that a bowling lane is not really "dry" in the truest sense of the word.

Bowling lanes actually are made up of two regions: the dry region and the wet region. The wet region is that part of the bowling lane that contains the oil pattern, while the dry region is just that part of the bowling lane that *doesn't* have any oil.

So, why do bowling alleys insist on putting oil on the boards? Well, since oil reduces friction, it's actually convenient to have some oil on a small region of the lane so as to facilitate the explosive rolling of the bowling ball. *After* the foul line, oil is usually present, so it's best to steer clear of the foul line at all times.

Never step on or beyond the foul line. The first reason is that it's against the standard rules, and second, as I said earlier, you will end up trailing oil all over the approach.

So, if there is oil before the foul line, you or someone else will eventually succumb to the oil. No one would like to fall flat on their back while carrying a sixteen pound bowling ball, remember that. No one will have fun if a member of your group has an accident while releasing a hook or straight shot.

Beginners are usually unaware that there are different kinds of oil patterns. It's good to know what kind of pattern is being used by your bowling center; it will help you to have a better strategy.

Different oil patterns bring distinct pros and cons. And as your teacher, it is my job to share with you how you can take advantage of different oil patterns, and how you can avoid the usual traps of the same.

Now, when you want to learn about oil patterns you have to be aware of the different sections of a bowling lane.

Bowling lanes have a definite number of wooden boards, and the spacing between these boards are consistent throughout the country. If you are playing a standard ten-pin bowling game, there is a good chance that your bowling lane also has standard measurements.

Let's lay down some definitions first, so you won't become confused:

Inside refers to the middle region of the bowling lane. It's the region usually utilized by most people when they are throwing balls, because there is a common belief that hitting pin # 1 will definitely send the others tumbling down.

Outside refers to that part of the bowling lane that is found directly next to the middle region. Outside can refer to either the left or right side of the lane.

Gutter refers to the canal that claims any wayward bowling balls. While playing bumper bowling, the gutter will be covered with some cushion that literally bumps the bowling ball back to the middle of the lane.

Now that you know what *inside, outside*, and *gutter* mean, let us move on to the first type of oil pattern. The first pattern is called the **house oil pattern**. The traits of the house oil pattern are as follows:

- It is the most common pattern used by bowling centers

- Widely used because the oil is concentrated on the inside

- Helps all novices hit their pins, even after a less than ideal throw

- Reduces the likelihood of gutter balls because there is less oil to tackle with

To improve your chances of having a good game with **house oil pattern**, try to remember the following guidelines:

- Be observant with your balls; do try to check how your bowling balls are behaving. It is very common for house oil patterns to be erratic. Some bowling center operators do this on purpose because they use this medium to try to find out what kind of oil volume is best suited for their diverse clientele.

- If extra buffing was performed on the last eight feet of the lane, it may be wise to use a dedicated bowling ball for hooks.

The next oil pattern is called the **chameleon oil pattern.** Here are the general characteristics of this oil pattern:

- Through its design, challenges the bowler to make adjustments based on his observation of the bowling lane

- Some regions of the lane will have more oil than others

- There is no fixed pattern and volume for the oil

- The oil is usually placed up to thirty-nine feet

In order to beat the chameleon oil pattern, you need to remember the following:

- Don't stick to just one part of the lane. The chameleon oil pattern was designed to frustrate players who become too complacent with their own techniques.

If you can't get your bowling ball to hook properly even with your best maneuvers, you can either move to the left or to the right of the lane, then try again.

- What's weird for you might end up being a completely normal play when the chameleon oil pattern is present. Step out of your comfort zone – you are not playing the house oil pattern. The chameleon oil pattern is not interested in delivering your bowling ball as quickly as possible to the pin deck.

- Versatility is the name of the game when using this pattern. Try to learn from others, and don't be afraid to discard your old techniques that just aren't working with the current bowling lane conditions.

The next pattern is **scorpion oil pattern**:

- This pattern features the highest volume of oil compared to all the other patterns that has been tackled thus far.

- A bowling lane using this pattern will have a high volume of oil, up to about forty-one feet.

- Requires more adaptation and agility.

In order to beat the scorpion oil pattern, you need to remember the following during play:

- Using old house balls will *not* work with the scorpion pattern. If you are serious about playing this oil pattern, get a set of reliable bowling balls. Get at least two, custom drilled balls – one for straight shots, and another one for hooks.

- Don't just dive into the game without knowing how your own balls will react to the heavy oil. At first, practice before you start your game. Be observant with some details such as: what part of the lane is better suited for hook shots? Which part of the lane accommodates straight shots? Learn, remember, and then adapt.

- If you want to outdo the oil, speed and power are of high importance. This becomes especially true if you like hook shots.

The next pattern is called the **shark oil pattern:**

- This is a moderately difficult pattern which has a moderate amount of oil on the bowling lane, up to forty-three feet. Although there is a high volume of oil, for some players, the distance covered by the oil can be problematic when they are used to having only thirty-nine feet of oil or less.

- This oil pattern discourages players from using the outside regions of the bowling lane which implies that you can't utilize the common boards that are easier for hooks and for delicate straight shots.

To beat this pattern, you have to do the following during play:

- Practice delivering the ball at the center of the lane
- Use the right ball for the game
- Learn to use tight angles for spares and strikes
- Practice straight shots that do not deviate from the target board

Mastering Spares

Half of the challenge is figuring out how to beat the lane's current oil pattern. After you must have mastered the oil pattern, you need to figure out how you can get the highest possible score per frame.

Every bowler dreams of the day that he can get a perfect 300 by simply throwing one brilliant strike after another.

In reality, the chances of this happening are really below 100%, so it would be best to stick to a more realistic approach. If you cannot get a strike, try to at least get a spare, and that is what we are going to talk about in this section of the book.

Here are some sage pieces of advice that will help you with spares:

- First, determine which ball in your arsenal is most likely to give you the most consistent strikes.

This is dependent by how you play generally, and what your particular strengths are when it comes to bowling. Once you have figured out which ball is your best bet when it comes to having to deliver strikes, move to the next item.

- Your starting position on the next ball should be determined by the orientation of the remaining pins. Do not leave anything to chance; don't think for a moment that you can make a bowling ball behave as if it was released five boards away.

If you have to move to the left or right as dictated by the position of the remaining pins, *move* and make the shot. If your remaining pins are dead center, approach from the center and knock them down.

- Keep in mind what kind of oil pattern has been used on the lane. Make adjustments, and if you have to use tight angles just to steer clear of the gutter, then do it.

- If you need to knock down the pins at the center of pin rack, *stay right* at the center and throw a straight shot.

- If pins 2 and 4 remain standing (these pins are located on the left side of the pin rack), then adjust your position. Move a maximum of five boards to the right, and then release a hook shot. This hook shot will snatch the errant pins easily.

- If you have two pins remaining on the right side of the pin deck (usually pins 6 and 9), do the opposite – move a few boards to the left. Some people think that just because the pins are on the left or right they have to stay *on* the same boards as the remaining pins.

Unless you are a wizard of straight shots who can easily beat the oil pattern, it is best to use hook shots to pick up these difficult spares.

- What if you have just one pin standing, and that pin is at the leftmost side (usually pin 7)? Instead of trying to skirt the bowling lane and pray that your ball doesn't fall into the gutter, do the opposite: quickly move a maximum of eight boards to the right of the target.

That's right: I am asking you to move eight boards, not four or five. Again, the goal here is to create a powerful hook shot that will pick up just *one* pin that is usually knocked down by surrounding pins.

- Do the same thing if you need to bring down the rightmost pin at the back, the 10 pins. You need to move to your left (eight boards worth) to hook down this errant little pin.

Adjustment Guidelines

Bowling is all about adaptation and adjustment. Not everyone is prepared for all the quite hard details, but I think you are almost quite ready. Here are some adjustment guidelines to help improve your gameplay:

1. If your shots are well-aimed and calculated, but you are still missing your intended targets, there is a possibility that you have to perform a lateral adjustment. Now it is of importance that you remember this: when you perform positional adjustments, you don't have to change your actual approach. All that changes are your position in relation to the lane and pins.

2. If you missed a pin on the right, you should make the appropriate lateral adjustment in that direction, so a few steps to the left or right will help you knock down those errant pins.

3. You can make as many lateral adjustments as you want depending on what kind of results you are getting with your bowling balls and the oil pattern of the lane.

4. If your bowling ball keeps missing its mark, or your balls are hooking too late, then consider moving forward or backward. If your bowling ball is hooking too early, move forward. If it is hooking too late, then

move backward so that your ball will have more time to curve at an angle.

5. If you are not very familiar with what kind of oil pattern is used in the bowling alley, forward or backward adjustments are often necessary.

You don't have to know the names of the oil pattern to master them. Just observe them and adapt – that is usually enough to produce a better game, trust me.

6. Speed of your ball definitely has an impact on the effectiveness of your shots. Ideally, your bowling ball should be able to disturb as many pins as possible to produce a strike based on its speed of acceleration.

So, if your ball is too fast, it will neatly knock down three pins and you will be left with seven untouched ones but if it doesn't have enough speed, it will hook at the wrong place and at the wrong time.

You can only adjust the speed of your ball by modifying your approach speed. Don't try to increase or decrease the speed of your bowling ball by muscling it around. Remember that your legs should be providing the momentum for the ball, and not your shoulder or arms.

7. Does your grip have an effect on the ball? Yes. If you want the ball to go straight, your fingers should be spread apart more than it should normally be and if you want the ball to spin and hook, then bring your fingers closer together.

References

History of Bowling
http://www.bowlingmuseum.com/Visit/HistoryofBowling.aspx [Accessed 20 Jan. 2013]

How to Choose the Right Bowling Ball
http://bowling.about.com/od/learntobowl/ht/howtochoosetherightball.htm [Accessed 20 Jan. 2013]

Plastic Bowling Balls
http://bowling.about.com/od/equipment/a/plastic_cover_stocks.htm [Accessed 20 Jan. 2013]

Bowling Pins
http://bowling.about.com/od/bowlingcenters/qt/bowling_pins.htm [Accessed 20 Jan. 2013]

Urethane Bowling Balls
http://bowling.about.com/od/equipment/a/urethane_cover_stocks.htm [Accessed 20 Jan. 2013]

Reactive Resin Bowling Balls
http://bowling.about.com/od/equipment/a/reactive_resin_cover_stocks.htm [Accessed 20 Jan. 2013]

Bowling Pin Rack
http://bowling.about.com/od/bowlingcenters/qt/pin_rack_dimensions.htm [Accessed 20 Jan. 2013]

How to Hold a Bowling Ball
http://bowling.about.com/od/learntobowl/qt/how-to-hold-a-bowling-ball.htm [Accessed 20 Jan. 2013]

Bowling Scoring

http://bowling.about.com/od/rulesofthegame/a/bowlingscoring.htm [Accessed 20 Jan. 2013]

How to Hook a Bowling Ball
http://bowling.about.com/od/learntobowl/ss/how_to_hook_a_bowling_ball_2.htm [Accessed 20 Jan. 2013]

Bumper Bowling
http://bowling.about.com/od/bowlingcenters/qt/Bumper-Bowling.htm [Accessed 20 Jan. 2013]

Bowling Etiquette
http://bowling.about.com/od/etiquette/qt/bowling_etiquette.htm [Accessed 20 Jan. 2013]

Why Does it Take 12 Strikes to Reach 300?
http://bowling.about.com/od/rulesofthegame/qt/Why-Does-It-Take-12-Strikes-To-Reach-300.htm [Accessed 20 Jan. 2013]

Conventional Grip
http://bowling.about.com/od/learntobowl/qt/conventional_grip.htm [Accessed 20 Jan. 2013]

Why Do You Have to Wear Bowling Shoes?
http://bowling.about.com/od/equipment/qt/Why-Do-You-Have-To-Wear-Bowling-Shoes.htm [Accessed 20 Jan. 2013]

How Often Should I Clean My Bowling Ball?
http://bowling.about.com/od/equipment/qt/How-Often-Should-I-Clean-My-Bowling-Ball.htm [Accessed 20 Jan. 2013]

House Oil Pattern

http://bowling.about.com/od/oilpatterns/p/house_oil_pattern.htm [Accessed 20 Jan. 2013]

Chameleon Oil Pattern
http://bowling.about.com/od/oilpatterns/p/chameleon_oil_pattern.htm [Accessed 20 Jan. 2013]

Scorpion Oil Pattern
http://bowling.about.com/od/oilpatterns/p/scorpion_oil_pattern.htm [Accessed 20 Jan. 2013]

Shark Oil Pattern
http://bowling.about.com/od/oilpatterns/p/shark_oil_pattern.htm [Accessed 20 Jan. 2013]

Viper Oil Pattern
http://bowling.about.com/od/oilpatterns/p/viper_oil_pattern.htm [Accessed 20 Jan. 2013]

Cheetah Oil Pattern
http://bowling.about.com/od/oilpatterns/p/cheetah_oil_pattern.htm [Accessed 20 Jan. 2013]

How to Pick Up Spares
http://bowling.about.com/od/learntobowl/ss/howtopickupspares_righties_9.htm [Accessed 20 Jan. 2013]

Lateral Adjustments
http://bowling.about.com/od/learntobowl/qt/adjustments_lateral.htm [Accessed 20 Jan. 2013]

Forward/Backward Adjustments
http://bowling.about.com/od/learntobowl/qt/adjustments_forward_backward.htm [Accessed 20 Jan. 2013]

Speed Adjustments
http://bowling.about.com/od/learntobowl/qt/adjustments_speed.htm [Accessed 20 Jan. 2013]

Finger Position Adjustments
http://bowling.about.com/od/learntobowl/qt/adjustments_finger_position.htm [Accessed 20 Jan. 2013]

Ball Adjustments
http://bowling.about.com/od/learntobowl/qt/adjustments_ball.htm [Accessed 20 Jan. 2013]

Don't Waste Strikes in Practice
http://bowling.about.com/od/learntobowl/qt/Wasting-Strikes-In-Practice.htm [Accessed 20 Jan. 2013]

Why am I Leaving the 7 Pin?
http://bowling.about.com/od/learntobowl/qt/Why-Am-I-Leaving-The-7-Pin.htm [Accessed 20 Jan. 2013]

Why am I Leaving the 10 Pin?
http://bowling.about.com/od/learntobowl/qt/Why-Am-I-Leaving-The-10-Pin.htm [Accessed 20 Jan. 2013]

Breaking Down Oil
http://bowling.about.com/od/oilpatterns/a/Breaking-Down-Oil.htm [Accessed 20 Jan. 2013]

Printed in Great Britain
by Amazon